Pla... H_2O

by C. M. Garrison

illustrated by Randy Chewning

Chapters

Harcourt

Orlando   Boston   Dallas   Chicago   San Diego

Visit *The Learning Site!*

www.harcourtschool.com

Earth from Space

The first Russian cosmonauts thought that the Earth looked like a big blue marble from outer space—a beautiful blue marble with swirling, white clouds. The blue they saw was all the water that covers the Earth. The

white clouds are water vapor. The clouds swirl because the wind pushes them.

Satellites take pictures of the Earth from space. They are used to help predict the weather. Satellite pictures can show all of us what the cosmonauts saw. With these pictures, we can see the outlines of the continents and how they are surrounded by water. Some of the Earth's largest lakes and rivers can also be seen from outer space.

H_2O is the chemical formula for what we call water. Scientists determine the formula for every substance on Earth.

Water is made up of two chemical elements:

hydrogen (H) and oxygen (O)

There are two hydrogen atoms to one oxygen atom. That's why the number 2 follows the H in the formula.

Pure water is colorless, odorless, and tasteless. Water is the most plentiful and important compound for the life of every animal and plant on Earth.

Water covers about 70 percent of the Earth's surface. When it freezes, it changes from a liquid to a solid. Water can also evaporate and become clouds. Then when it rains or snows, the water returns to Earth. Water often changes form, but the total amount of water on our planet never changes.

Water can exist in three forms:
gaseous—clouds in the atmosphere
liquid—the water we drink
solid—ice

The Three Types of Water on Earth

1. *vapor* water in the form of clouds
2. *surface* lakes, rivers, streams, oceans
3. *ground* underground sources that provide water for drinking

About 97 percent of the water on Earth is salty. This water is in oceans and seas. The remaining 3 percent of the Earth's water, in the form of ice, snow, or liquid-water, is found on land, in rivers and lakes, and underground.

We all need water to live. Humans can live much longer without food than without water.

5 The water drops become heavy and fall as rain or snow.

4 The drops of water come together and form clouds.

3 The water vapor condenses, or changes into tiny drops of water.

2 This gas, or water vapor, meets cool air.

6 The rain and melted snow flow into streams, lakes, and oceans.

1 The sun's heat makes water evaporate, or change into a gas.

The *water cycle* shows how water changes form and location as it travels between the air, the land, and the ocean. It is an endless movement.

The water cycle is how water is returned to the Earth after it evaporates. When scientists figured out how the water cycle works, it was a true breakthrough. This knowledge has helped people around the world understand how to take good care of our water resources.

Huge chunks of snow and ice fall into Prince William Sound.

A Closer Look

Glaciers

Many thousands of years ago huge ice sheets covered all of Canada and what is now the northern part of the United States. These great sheets of ice are known as *glaciers*.

Glaciers are rivers of ice that move and push dirt and rocks. When glaciers melt and move, they change the land. Glaciers cut valleys through the land, make rolling hills, and create rivers, lakes, and ponds.

Today glaciers are found only in extremely cold areas and on high mountains.

You can tell where a glacier has been by the signs it has left behind. Sometimes you may notice strange rocks in a field or a lake that don't match the others. These rocks were probably brought to that spot by glaciers. Large cuts in rocks are most likely scratches made by the ice from a glacier.

You can visit a glacier! Many people take cruise ships to Alaska to see the moving glacier dumping great chunks of ice and snow into the ocean. In Jasper, Canada, you can actually ride out onto a glacial field. The large snow buses take you to the great ice fields, where you can look down into very deep holes in the ice.

Oceans and Seas

Sailing on one of the world's great *oceans* has always been an adventure. For hundreds of years, sailors have told many stories about sea monsters and strange lands.

There are five great oceans on Earth and seven major seas. The largest ocean is the Pacific. It covers an area of 70 million square miles! It is also the deepest ocean on Earth. The deepest part of the Pacific Ocean is 36,000 feet deep. That's over 7 miles. The tallest mountain on Earth is Mt. Everest, and it's only 6 miles high. An altimeter is used to measure how tall and deep mountains and oceans are.

Columbus disregarded the idea that the Earth was flat. He sailed across the Atlantic Ocean in search of India. He returned somewhat dejectedly when he had found America and not India.

Oceans and seas have very strong waves that crash on the land. The crashing waves smooth out coastlines.

A *sea* is different from an ocean. A sea is a part of an ocean, which is a bigger body of water. A sea is also partly surrounded by land. For example, the Caribbean Sea is surrounded by Florida, Cuba, and many little islands.

All oceans and seas have salt water. Salt is a mineral that is found in soil and rocks. Flowing water picks up the salt and carries it to rivers. Rivers carry the salt to the seas. This has been happening for millions of years. The oceans have a lot of salt—about one cup per gallon.

Did you ever wonder why oceans are blue? Scientists have different ideas about that. Some think it's because the sunlight reflects on the seawater, making it appear blue.

The Nile River, in Africa, is the world's longest river. It is 4,160 miles long.

Rivers and Lakes

Rivers can be found everywhere. Some are small enough for a person to jump over. Others are so large that they look almost like lakes.

A river carries a lot of water. Gravity makes the water flow downhill to the ocean. Rivers start out as streams and get bigger as they get closer to the ocean.

Some rivers don't make it to the ocean. Some rivers end up in lakes. Some seem to disappear into the ground or into marshes.

Springs that bubble up through the ground are the source of most rivers.

Some rivers' sources are melting snow and glaciers.

Rivers can be dammed up to create lakes. These lakes can be used for fishing, boating, and swimming. The water from these lakes is also used for drinking and for watering crops.

The water released from a dam can be used to create electricity. The rushing water turns engines that create the power. The power is then sent through electric lines so people can light their homes.

Some dams are made of earth and stone. The largest dams are made of steel and cement.

Hoover Dam controls the flow of the Colorado River. The dam created Lake Havasu and provides electricity for Los Angeles, California.

Lakes are used for fishing, swimming, and boating.

A *lake* is surrounded by land, and the water in it doesn't flow. Rivers are the sources of most lakes. The river comes in one end of the lake and goes out the other. This new water helps keep the lake water fresh. Rainfall on lakes also helps keep their water levels high. Lakes can dry up if there isn't enough water to feed them.

Most lakes are natural. Some are made by humans. The largest lake in the world is the Caspian Sea in central Asia. It's called a sea because it's so big. The United States also has some very large lakes. They are called the Great Lakes. One of these lakes, Lake Superior, is the second-largest lake in the world.

Marshes and Swamps

Marshes and *swamps* are very wet, muddy places. In these places, the ground is covered with shallow water. In marshes, weeds and plants grow up through the water. Trees can grow in the water of swamps.

Marshes and swamps are known as *wetlands*. Wetlands are home to many different fish, birds, and animals. Some wetlands in the United States are protected. This means the animals there will always have a safe place to live. However, many wetlands are not protected and are endangered.

The Everglades in Florida is the world's largest marsh. It covers an area of 4,000 square miles.

Water dripping in underground caves creates strange rock formations.

Groundwater

Underground water is called *groundwater*. Wells must be dug to get this water. The water is then pumped from the wells to farms, homes, and factories.

There is a lot of groundwater. Rain seeps down into the soil and is cleaned as it goes through layers of rocks. Because it has been filtered by rocks and sand, underground water is usually very clean.

Even though there is a great deal of groundwater, we must be careful not to use too much of it. We also need to be sure that poisons aren't put into our groundwater. Chemicals from factories and sprays for crops can poison the water supply.

What Water Means to Us

Water is the most important and plentiful thing on our beautiful, big, blue planet. Every living thing on Earth needs water to survive. If we are careful to keep it clean, it will continue to support life for all of us.